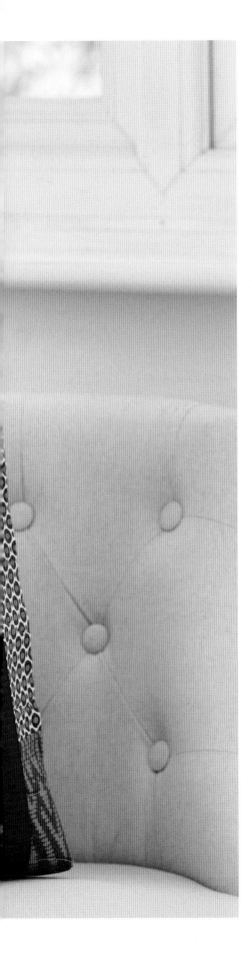

CONTENTS

P9-DNY-781

Introduction

Different bags are needed for shopping, working, holidaying or just to look stylish. Here you will find ten different patterns each for a different purpose.

I have chosen fresh, bright fabrics with simple but stunning patchwork designs. Patchwork involves using two or more fabrics with a number of shaped pieces. Some bags feature squares, triangles or rectangles in a variety of patterns making the patchwork a real focal point. Each project includes sewing instructions, step-by-step photos and handy hints.

Projects are graded as either 'Easy' or 'Requires experience'. Basic sewing skills are needed for the 'Easy' projects and are suitable for beginners. The 'Requires experience' projects have more steps and will take a little longer to make. There are no pattern pieces as most of the bags are made from geometric shapes that can be cut simply with a rotary cutter or scissors.

Sections on patchwork and bag making techniques can be found at the back of the book and I suggest that you read these through first before beginning. These provide a really good starting point and describe all the basics in detail.

Enjoy making and using your very own bags.

Janet Goddard

MEASUREMENTS

All the cutting instructions for these projects include a 0.75cm (¼in) seam allowance. I have used metric as the standard measurement throughout all my patterns but the imperial measurements have been included as well. Please use either centimetres or inches but do not mix the two together.

FABRIC AND THREAD

One of the nicest parts of starting a new project is being able to choose the fabrics. I have made fabric choices to suit the bag pattern. If the bag is large I have tended to use fabric that has a bigger pattern and for smaller bags the fabric pattern has tended to be smaller as well.

All of the bags in this book use fabric that is 100 per cent cotton and of a high-quality. Bags need to be robust and hard-wearing, and I think if you skimp on the quality of the fabric, the wear and tear shows through more quickly.

The fabrics used for the bags in this book are bright and modern and incredibly varied. They have been chosen to suit the design of the bag and for the purpose intended.

The fabric allowances in the patterns are for fabric that is approximately 107cm (42in) wide from selvedge to selvedge. I always cut the selvedges from the fabric before beginning a project and rarely pre-wash the fabrics, but this is personal choice. Each pattern details the fabric colourway and print that I have used but you can substitute your own fabric to suit.

The fabric allowances in each pattern allow for 5 – 7.5cm (2 – 3in) extra so if a small mistake is made here and there you shouldn't run out of fabric, but do try to be as careful as possible.

The best thread for patchwork and bag making is high-quality cotton thread. I tend to use a grey coloured thread for all construction unless I am topstitching or quilting. If I am topstitching I try and use a thread that matches the fabric to be topstitched and this would usually be a cotton thread. Some of the bags are machine quilted and here I may use a synthetic thread that has a sheen to it in order to showcase the quilting.

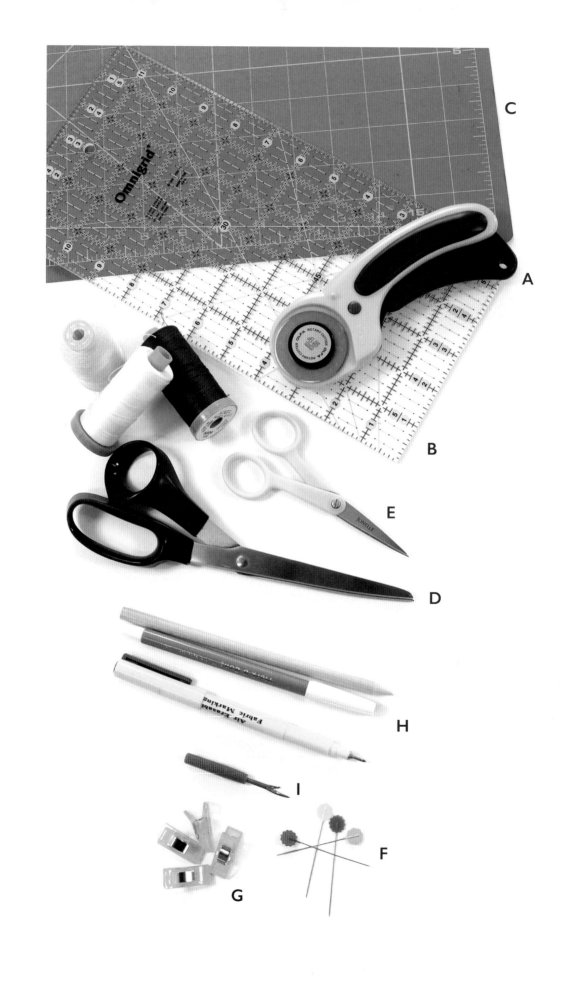

C

A

B

E

D

H

I

F

G

EQUIPMENT

Good quality basic equipment is needed. There is no need to spend a fortune on the latest gadgets, just invest in some good quality essential resources.

Sewing machine: The most important piece of equipment for bag making and patchwork is a sewing machine. It really only needs to be able to stitch forwards and backwards and doesn't need a whole lot of fancy stitches. It is important that your machine is cared for and is cleaned and serviced regularly to keep it working well. A little oil applied according to the manufacturer's instructions should help to keep everything in good order. Changing the needle regularly also helps with the quality of stitching and I usually change the needle on the machine every time I begin a new project. The two machine feet used the most are the 0.75cm (¼in) patchwork foot which is excellent for maintaining 0.75cm (¼in) wide seams, and the walking foot used for machine quilting.

Rotary cutter, ruler and mat: All the pieces for the bag projects in this book can be cut using a rotary cutter (A), ruler (B) and a rotary cutting mat (C). A rotary cutter is a cutting instrument with a round-wheeled blade. This is used with an acrylic ruler and a self-healing cutting mat.

A good quality rotary cutter should have a protective safety shield on it that can be pushed on and off. It is important to train yourself to always make sure that the safety cover is on the blade every time the cutter is put down. Blades are sharp and can cut through up to eight layers of fabric at a time so can do a lot of damage to hands if not kept safe. Replace the blades when they start to become blunt.

Rulers come in many shapes and sizes, are marked in centimetres or inches and are made of tough acrylic. I personally find the rulers with yellow markings the easiest to see on fabric but it is a personal choice. If you are purchasing just one ruler make it a 15 x 61cm (6 x 24in) ruler as this can be used for most projects.

A rotary cutting mat is a self-healing mat designed to be used with a rotary cutter. Mats come with grid markings on them which can be used with the ruler for accurate cutting. If you are purchasing a mat for the first time buy the largest you can afford. A 61 x 91cm (24 x 36in) mat is a good investment.

Scissors: A good sharp pair of dress-making scissors (D) is essential for tasks such as cutting off corners, cutting curves or cutting through cotton webbing. A small pair (E) is also handy for snipping threads and curved seams.

Pins: I use flat flowerhead fine pins (F) for patchwork as they help to keep the fabric flat but any type of pins will do.

Needles: Hand-sewing needles are used for some finishing off techniques and are available in many sizes. Sharps are good for general sewing but an embroidery needle is useful for thicker thread when stitching on leather handles.

Clips: (G) These are a recent addition to the sewing world but are just great for bag making as they hold multiple layers of fabric together especially on curved seams. The clips are plastic (think mini clothes pegs but better) and can be removed easily as you stitch with the machine.

Fabric markers: There are many fabric markers (H) available but any marker should be easy to use, easy to see and simple to remove after you have finished sewing. Markers are used to mark measurements for cutting or stitching and also quilting lines or patterns. Several different markers are needed in order to contrast with both light and dark fabrics. White and silver markers, water-erasable pens and charcoal markers are all useful.

Seam ripper: (I) This is often called a 'quick unpick' and usually comes as a tool with the sewing machine. Hugely useful for removing tacking (basting) stitches or the odd mistake we all make now and then.

Iron and ironing board: After the sewing machine the iron is the most useful tool in patchwork and bag making. A press with a dry iron is all that is needed and the use of a good quality iron does make a difference to the finished product. The ironing surface needs to be firm and clean.

Projects

10 modern patchwork bag designs.

Shopper's Tote Bag

A roomy bag for the serious shopper.

A roomy bag for the serious shopper.

Size: 41 × 46 × 13cm (16 × 18 × 5in) excluding handles

SKILL LEVEL: EASY

This is a go anywhere shopping bag which is a good size and sturdy enough to carry all that shopping. The strong handles curve around under the bag to give it extra support so it can carry heavier items. The bright, modern fabric choices will lighten up even the dullest day and put a zing in your step when you are out shopping.

MATERIALS

FABRIC
- 1m (40in) red patterned fabric for the outer bag base and lining
- 38cm (15in) flower print for the outer bag centre panels
- 38cm (15in) dotty fabric for the outer bag side panels

WADDING (BATTING)
- 53cm (20in) fusible wadding or a firmer lining product if desired

HABERDASHERY
- 3m × 2.5cm (120 × 1in) wide navy blue cotton webbing for the handles

CUTTING

All cutting instructions include a 0.75cm (¼in) seam allowance.

For any directional fabric ensure that the fabric is cut carefully so that the pattern is facing the correct way up.

Red patterned fabric
- one 48 x 35.5cm (19 x 14in) rectangle for the base
- one 48 x 99cm (19 x 39in) rectangle for the lining

Flower print fabric
- two 23 x 33cm (9 x 13in) rectangles for the outer bag centre panels

Dotty fabric
- four 14 x 33cm (5½ x 13in) rectangles for the outer bag side panels

Fusible wadding (batting)
- one 46 x 96.5cm (18 x 38in) rectangle for the lining

STEP BY STEP

TO STITCH THE OUTER BAG:

1. Stitch a 14 x 33cm (5½ x 13in) dotty fabric rectangle to each side of a 23 x 33cm (9 x 13in) flower print rectangle. Press seams towards the centre panel.

2. Stitch each of the panels made in step 1 to the 48 x 35.5cm (19 x 14in) red patterned base panel. If using directional fabric ensure that the pattern is facing upwards away from the base (**A**).

(A)

3. Iron the fusible wadding (batting) to the wrong side of the outer bag.

4. Quilt in horizontal wavy lines, approximately 5cm (2in) apart across the outer bag.

TO STITCH THE HANDLES:

5. For the handles, take the cotton webbing and starting in the middle of the outer bag base lay the webbing so that it covers the first seam between the side and front panel, continue so the handle loops 53cm (20in) above the top of the bag, and then make sure it covers the side seam on the other side. The webbing then goes across the outer bag base and up the seam on the other side of the bag, loops 53cm (20in) on the top of this side and back down the seam line, meeting at the point where it started. Pin the webbing in place. Topstitch each side of the webbing in place stopping 6.5cm (2½in) from the top of the bag on each handle.

TO STITCH THE LINING:

6. Fold the 48 x 99cm (19 x 39in) rectangle of red lining fabric in half and stitch down each side leaving a 13cm (5in) opening in one side.

7. To shape the base of the lining, match the base seam with the side seam. Measure in 7cm (2¾in) along the seam line and stitch across. Cut off the excess fabric (**B**). Repeat on the other corner.

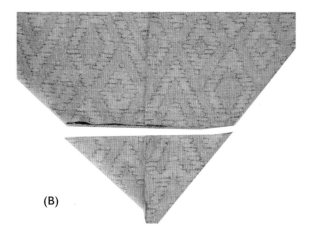

(B)

TO STITCH THE BAG TOGETHER:

8. Fold the outer bag right sides together and stitch down each side ensuring that the handles are kept out of the way of the stitching.

9. To shape the base of the outer bag follow the instructions in step 7 for the lining. Turn the bag right sides out.

10. Place the outer bag inside the lining so that the right side of the lining is facing the right side of the bag. Match the side seams and pin in place. Keep the handles pushed well down. Stitch around the top.

11. Turn the bag through the opening in the lining and stitch the opening closed. Press gently to remove any creases.

12. Stitch 0.75cm (¼ in) around the top edge of the bag.

13. Pin the loose part of each handle up to the top of the bag. Topstitch along each edge of the webbing and across the top, stitching through the outer bag and the lining.

HANDY HINTS:

• I have used a firmer lining product in this bag than the usual fusible wadding (batting) to give the bag a good degree of stability. It does make the bag much thicker than usual so doesn't work for smaller, more delicate bags.

• I have used cotton webbing for the handles on this bag but the webbing could be substituted for some co-ordinating fabric handles.

Summertime Bucket Bag

A large bag for summer day trips or shopping.

A large bag for summer day trips or shopping.

Size: 53 × 38 × 10cm (21 × 15 × 4in) excluding handles

SKILL LEVEL: REQUIRES EXPERIENCE

A large go-anywhere bag that will hold a mountain of stuff whether it is all the essentials for a day out or a trip to the shops. The summery fabric choice and pastel shades coupled with the elegant leather handles give the bag a sophisticated air. The flying geese patchwork provide a good focal point to the centre of the bag. I can't wait to make lots more!

MATERIALS

FABRIC

- 75cm (30in) floral print for the outer bag
- 75cm (30in) green print for the lining and inner pocket
- 63.5cm (25in) yellow print for the patchwork and bag base

(These fabric quantities allow for using a directional print.)

WADDING (BATTING)

- 56cm (24in) fusible wadding

HABERDASHERY

- 13cm (5in) Vilene Decovil (Pellon Decor Bond) or similar for the bag base
- four bag studs/feet
- one set of 58cm (23in) leather piped bag handles
- thick embroidery thread for stitching on the handles

CUTTING

All cutting instructions include 0.75cm (¼in) seam allowance.

Floral print
- four 25 × 31.5cm (9¾ × 12½in) rectangles for the outer bag
- two 5 × 58.5cm (2 × 23in) strips for the outer bag
- twelve 7.4cm (2⅞in) squares for the patchwork

Green print
- two 47 × 58.5cm (18½ × 23in) rectangles for the lining
- 15 × 51cm (6 × 20in) rectangle for the pocket

Yellow print
- two 13 × 58.5cm (5 × 23in) rectangles for the bag base
- three 13.5cm (5¼in) squares for the patchwork

Fusible wadding (batting)
- two 56 × 46cm (22 × 18in) rectangles for the bag lining

Vilene Decovil (or similar) interfacing
- one 10 × 28cm (4 × 11in) rectangle for the bag base

STEP BY STEP

TO STITCH THE PATCHWORK:

1. Draw a line on the diagonal from corner to corner on the wrong side of the twelve 7.4cm (2⅞in) floral print squares (**A**).

2. Position two 7.4cm (2⅞in) squares on diagonally opposite corners of a 13.5cm (5¼in) yellow print square right sides facing. Stitch a seam 0.75cm (¼in) away from each side of the drawn line.

 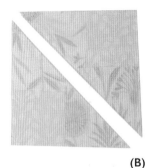

(A)   (B)

3. Cut along the drawn line (**B**) and press seams towards the small triangles (**C**).

4. Position another 7.4cm (2⅞in) floral print square on the remaining unsewn corner of each unit so that the diagonal line is positioned between the two smaller triangles. Stitch a seam 0.75cm (¼in) away from each side of the drawn line (**D**).

(C)   (D)

5. Cut along the drawn line (**E**) and press seams towards the small triangles (**F**). Trim points (**G**). Continue in this way until twelve triangle units are stitched. Each unit should measure 6.5 × 11.5cm (2½ × 4½in).

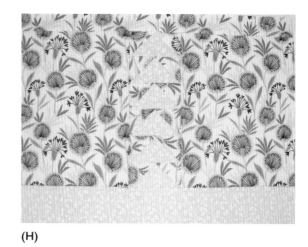

(H)

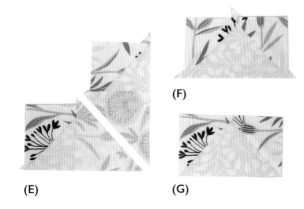

(F)

(E) (G)

TO STITCH THE OUTER BAG:

6. Stitch the patchwork triangle units into two strips of 6 triangles. Press seams towards the base of the triangles.

7. Take the strips of patchwork triangles and stitch a 25 × 31.5cm (9¾ × 12½in) floral print rectangle to each side. Press the seams away from the patchwork.

8. Stitch a 5 × 58.5cm (2 × 23in) strip of floral print to the top of each of the outer bag pieces completed in step 7, pressing seams towards the strip. Stitch a 13 × 58.5cm (5 × 23in) yellow print rectangle to the bottom of each of the outer bag pieces, pressing seams towards the base (**H**). You have completed two outer bag pieces.

9. Iron a 56 × 46cm (22 × 18in) rectangle of fusible wadding (batting) to the wrong side of each outer bag piece. The wadding will be smaller than the outer bag at the top and bottom of the bag so that there will not be any bulky seams.

10. To create the bucket shape to the bag, mark 10cm (4in) from the outer edge at the bottom of each outer bag piece. Place a ruler on the very outer edge at the top on the right side of the bag and on the 10cm (4in) marking at the bottom of the bag. Cut the wedge shape of fabric away. Repeat on all corners of the outer bag pieces.

11. Place the outer bag panels together, right sides facing, and stitch down each side and across the bottom, leaving the top open.

12. To shape the base of the bag, match the centre fold of the base with the side seam. Measure in 4.5cm (1¾in) along the seam line and stitch across. Cut off the excess fabric. Repeat on the other corner. Turn the bag right side out.

13. Place the 10 x 28cm (4 x 11in) rectangle of Vilene Decovil in the base of the outer bag and press carefully, making sure that you do not catch the iron on the wadding (batting).

14. To add the bag studs, measure in 2.5cm (1in) from each corner and carefully make a small hole with a seam ripper. Press the stud from the right side of the fabric through the base of the bag and open the teeth out. Repeat for all four studs.

TO STITCH THE LINING:

15. To stitch the pocket take the 15 x 51cm (6 x 20in) green print rectangle and fold in half, wrong sides together, so that the top edge measures 25.5cm (10in). Stitch around the three raw edges, leaving a 7.6cm (3in) opening. Trim corners, turn right sides out, and press.

16. Position the completed pocket on one of the 47 x 58.5cm (18½ x 23in) green print rectangles for the lining, 10cm (4in) from the top. Topstitch down each side and across the bottom leaving the top edge open. Topstitch down the middle of the pocket to create two compartments.

17. Following the instructions in step 10 cut two lining pieces into bucket shapes (**I**).

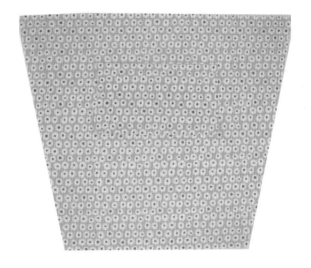

18. Place the lining panels right sides together and stitch down each side and across the bottom, leaving a 13cm (5in) gap for turning in one side and leaving the top open. Shape the bottom of the lining in the same way as the outer bag bottom in step 12.

TO STITCH THE BAG TOGETHER:

19. Keeping the bag right sides out and the lining wrong sides out, place the outer bag inside the lining (**J**).

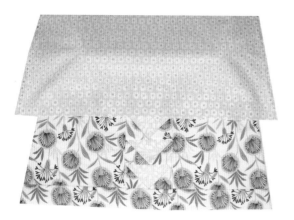

(J)

20. Matching the side seams, stitch around the top edge of the bag.

21. Turn the bag through the opening and stitch the opening in the lining closed. Carefully press the top of the bag so that the lining matches the top edge of the outer bag. Topstitch around the edge.

22. Using thick embroidery thread stitch the leather handles to the top of the bag.

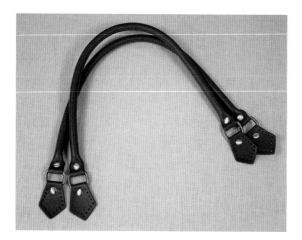

HANDY HINTS:

• When stitching the handles to the top of the bag position them so that they are at an appropriate width for whoever will be using the bag. This will vary if the bag is to be used as a shoulder bag or carried by hand.

• My bag is not quilted, but if you would like to add quilting do this after step 10.

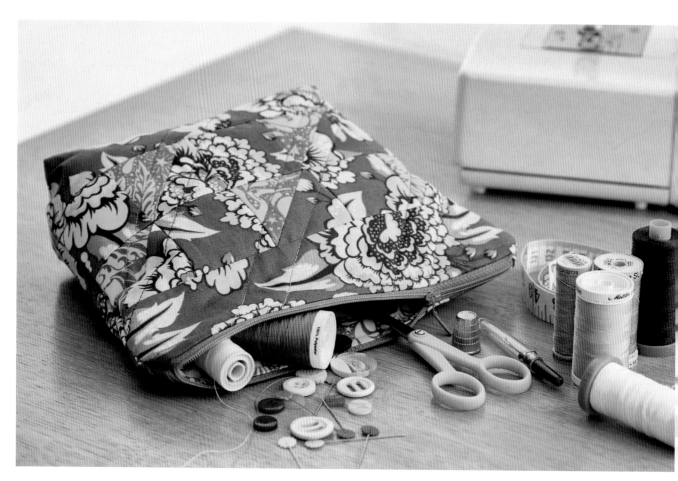

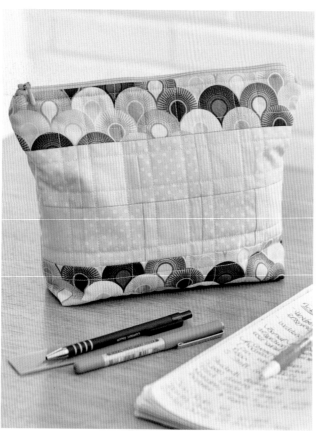

A Trio of Pouches

Handy pouches for everyday use.

Handy pouches for everyday use.

Size: 25.5 × 18 × 7.5cm (10 × 7 × 3in)

SKILL LEVEL: EASY

Super useful, medium-sized pouches for cosmetics, toiletries, sewing supplies or even stationery. There are three patchwork designs to choose from – rectangles, squares or triangles or make one of each! These would make lovely gifts for friends or family and can be stitched together quite quickly. Who could resist such a pretty handmade gift?

MATERIALS (Pouch with patchwork rectangles)

FABRIC
- 38cm (15in) turquoise floral fabric for the patchwork and lining
- 20.5cm (8in) pink spot fabric for the main pouch
- 15cm (6in) fan print fabric for the patchwork

WADDING (BATTING)
- 30cm (12in) fusible wadding

HABERDASHERY
- one 30cm (12in) pink zip

CUTTING

All cutting instructions include a 0.75cm (¼in) seam allowance.

Turquoise floral fabric
- two 24 × 28cm (9½ × 11in) rectangles for the lining
- eight 5 × 11.5cm (2 × 4½in) rectangles for the patchwork

Pink spot fabric
- two 6.5 × 28cm (2½ × 11in) rectangles for the outer pouch
- two 9 × 28cm (3½ × 11in) rectangles for the outer pouch

Fan print fabric
- six 5 × 11.5cm (2 × 4½in) rectangles for the patchwork

Fusible wadding (batting)
- two 24 × 28cm (9½ × 11in) rectangles for the lining

STEP BY STEP

TO STITCH THE PATCHWORK:
1. Take the fourteen 5 × 11.5cm (2 × 4½in) turquoise and fan print rectangles and stitch them into two strips of seven rectangles with the fabrics alternating (**A**). Press seams in one direction.

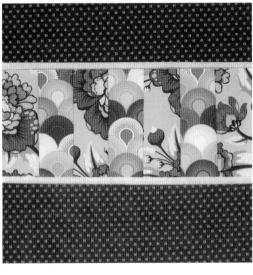

(A)

TO STITCH THE OUTER POUCH AND LINING:
2. Take the two patchwork strips and stitch a 6.5 × 28cm (2½ × 11in) pink spot rectangle to the top of each strip and a 9 × 28cm (3½ × 11in) pink spot rectangle to the bottom of each strip (**A**). Press seams away from the patchwork. You now have two outer pouch sections.

3. Iron the fusible wadding (batting) to the wrong sides of each of the two outer pouch sections.

4. Machine quilt each of the outer pouch sections by stitching vertical lines 1cm (½in) apart from top to bottom (**B**).

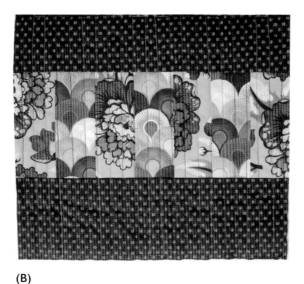

(B)

5. To attach the zip, place the first outer pouch section right side up and place the zip face down on front of it, aligning the top edge. Place the lining right side down and stitch along the top edge to secure the lining, zip and outer pouch (**C**).

(C)

6. Repeat for the second pouch section.

7. Open out and press. Stitch 0.75cm (¼in) each side of the zip (**D**).

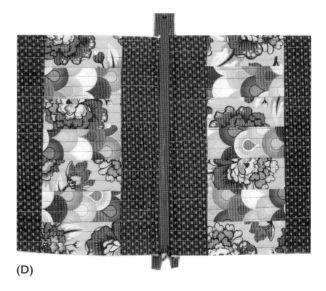

(D)

8. Open the zip half way (this is very important). Place the two outer pouch sections and the lining panels right sides together. Pin (**E**) and stitch all the way around the edge, leaving a 7.5cm (3in) gap in the bottom of the lining.

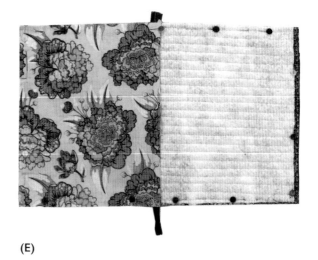

(E)

9. To shape the base match the centre fold of the base with the side seam. Measure in 1½in (4cm) along the seam line and stitch across. Cut off the excess fabric. Repeat on the other corner and also all the lining corners.

10. Turn the pouch right sides out through the gap in the lining and stitch the gap closed.

MATERIALS (Pouch with patchwork triangles)

FABRIC
- 38cm (15in) turquoise fabric for the patchwork and lining
- 35.5cm (14in) grey floral fabric for the main pouch

WADDING (BATTING)
- 30cm (12in) fusible wadding

HABERDASHERY
- one 30cm (12in) grey zip

CUTTING
All cutting instructions include a 0.75cm (¼in) seam allowance.

Turquoise floral fabric
- two 24 x 28cm (9½ x 11in) rectangles for the lining
- five 7.4cm (2⅞in) squares for the patchwork

Grey floral fabric
- two 6.5 x 28cm (2½ x 11in) rectangles for the outer pouch
- two 9 x 28cm (3½ x 11in) rectangles for the outer pouch

- five 7.4cm (2⅞in) squares for the patchwork
- ten 6.5cm (2½in) squares for the patchwork
- four 2.5 x 11.5cm (1 x 4½in) strips for the outer pouch

Fusible wadding (batting)
- two 24 x 28cm (9½ x 11in) rectangles for the lining

STEP BY STEP

TO STITCH THE PATCHWORK:

1. Draw a line on the diagonal, on the reverse of all the 7.4cm (2⅞in) turquoise squares (**A**).

2. Place each turquoise square right sides together on a 7.4cm (2⅞in) grey square. Stitch 0.75cm (¼in) on each side of the diagonal line. Cut on the drawn diagonal line (**B**). Press seams towards the darker fabric to finish the squares (**C**).

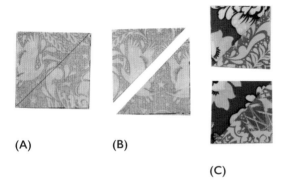

(A)   (B)

(C)

3. For each outer pouch side you will need five of the triangle units made in step 2 and five 6.5cm (2½in) grey floral squares. The first row will have three triangles and two squares alternating with each other and the second row will have three squares and two triangles alternating with each other. Stitch each row and then stitch the two rows together. Press the seams in the rows in alternate directions.

TO STITCH THE OUTER POUCH AND LINING:

4. Take the two units stitched in step 3 and stitch a 2.5 x 11.5cm (1 x 4½in) grey turquoise strip to each end. Press seams towards the patchwork.

5. Stitch a 6.5 x 28cm (2½ x 11in) grey floral rectangle to the top of the patchwork and a 9 x 28cm (3½ x 11in) grey floral rectangle to the bottom of the patchwork following (**D**). Press seams away from the patchwork. You now have two outer pouch sections.

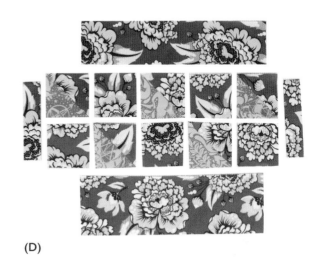

(D)

6. Iron the fusible wadding (batting) to the reverse of the two outer pouch sections.

7. Machine quilt each of the outer pouch sections by stitching in random diagonal lines (**E**).

(E)

8. To finish the pouch, follow steps 5 to 10 for the pouch with patchwork rectangles.

MATERIALS (Pouch with patchwork squares)

FABRIC

- 35.5cm (14in) pink plain fabric for the patchwork and lining
- 20.5cm (8in) fan print fabric for the main pouch
- 10cm (4in) green spot fabric for the patchwork

WADDING (BATTING)

- 30cm (12in) fusible wadding

HABERDASHERY

- one 30cm (12in) pink zip

CUTTING

All cutting instructions include a 0.75cm (¼in) seam allowance.

Pink plain fabric

- two 24 × 28cm (9½ × 11in) rectangles for the lining
- ten 6.5cm (2½in) squares for the patchwork

Fan print fabric

- two 6.5 × 28cm (2½ × 11in) rectangles for the outer pouch
- two 9 × 28cm (3½ × 11in) rectangles for the outer pouch
- four 2.5 × 11.5cm (1 × 4½in) strips for the outer pouch

Green spot fabric

- ten 6.5cm (2½in) squares for the patchwork

Fusible wadding (batting)

- two 24 × 28cm (9½ × 11in) rectangles for the lining

STEP BY STEP

TO STITCH THE PATCHWORK:

1. For each outer pouch side you will need five 6.5cm (2½in) pink squares and five 6.5cm (2½in) green spot squares. Arrange the squares into two rows of five so that the fabrics alternate in colour.

2. Stitch each row and then stitch the two rows together. Press the seams in the rows in alternate directions.

TO STITCH THE OUTER POUCH AND LINING:

3. Take the two units stitched in step 2 and stitch a 2.5 × 11.5cm (1 × 4½in) fan print strip to each end. Press seams towards the patchwork.

4. Stitch a 6.5 × 28cm (2½ × 11in) fan print rectangle to the top of the patchwork and a 9 × 28cm (3½ × 11in) fan print rectangle to the bottom of the patchwork. Press seams away from the patchwork. You now have two outer pouch sections.

5. Iron the fusible wadding (batting) to the wrong side of each of the two outer pouch sections.

6. Machine quilt each of the outer pouch sections by stitching horizontal and vertical lines 1.5cm (½in) away from each seam line (**A**).

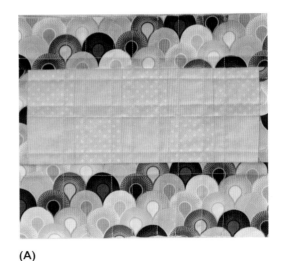

(A)

7. To finish the pouch, follow steps 5 to 10 for the pouch with patchwork rectangles.

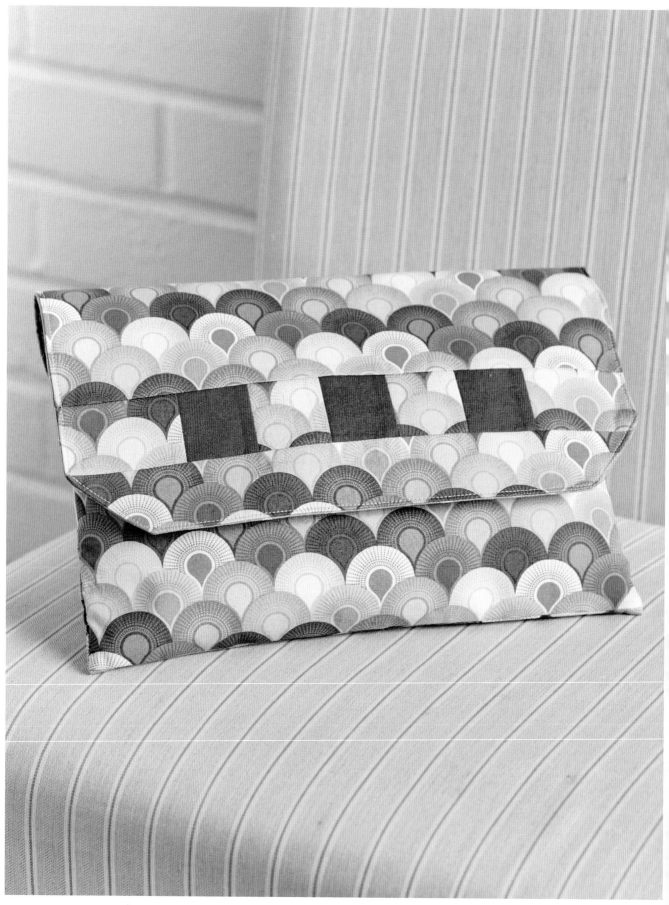

Classic Clutch Bag

A stylish addition to any outfit.

A stylish addition to any outfit.

Size: 30 x 20.5cm (12 x 8in)

SKILL LEVEL: EASY

A compact classic clutch will add an air of elegance to a special outfit or occasion. The clutch is roomy enough for carrying all those essentials, with a padded quilted lining and a firm exterior which will maintain its shape. The luxurious fan-patterned fabric with the contrasting plain red fabric makes this a very special bag. Try making this in a fabric to match a dress or jacket you wear for those special occasions.

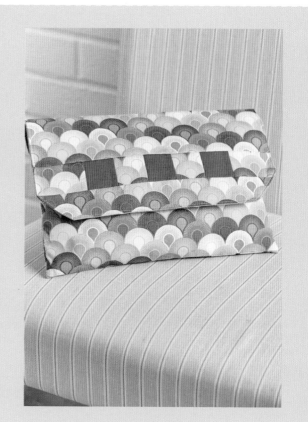

MATERIALS

FABRIC
- 35.5cm (14in) fan print fabric for the outer bag
- 35.5cm (14in) green spot fabric for the lining
- 5cm (3in) red plain fabric for the patchwork

WADDING (BATTING)/INTERFACING
- 35.5cm (14in) fusible wadding
- 35.5cm (14in) firm fusible interfacing

HABERDASHERY
- one magnetic snap

CUTTING

All cutting instructions include a
0.75cm (¼in) seam allowance.

Fan print fabric

- one 16.5 x 33cm (6½ x 13in) piece for
  the bag front
- one 11.5 x 33cm (4½ x 13in) piece for
  the top flap
- one 5 x 33cm (2 x 13in) piece for the
  bottom flap
- two 9.5 x 33cm (3¾ x 13in) pieces for
  the back
- four 5 x 7.5cm (2 x 3in) rectangles
  for the patchwork front and back
- four 5cm (2in) squares for the
  patchwork front and back

Green spot fabric

- one 33 x 54.5cm (13 x 21½ in) piece for
  the lining

Red plain fabric

- six 5cm (2in) squares for the front and
  back patchwork

Fusible wadding (batting)

- one 31.5 x 56cm (12½ x 21in) piece for
  the lining

Firm fusible interfacing

- one 33 x 54.5cm (13 x 21½in) piece for
  the outer bag

STEP BY STEP

TO STITCH THE PATCHWORK:

1. Take two 5cm (2in) fan print squares,
three 5cm (2in) red plain squares and two
5 x 7.5cm (2 x 3in) fan print rectangles and
stitch together so that a rectangle is on each
end and the red squares are alternated with
fan print squares (**A**). Press seams. Repeat
with the remaining squares and rectangles to
make two patchwork strips.

(A)

TO STITCH THE OUTER BAG:

2. If using a directional fabric make sure
the fabric will face the same way as in (**A**).
Stitch the fabric pieces and patchwork strips
together along each of the long edges, in
this order:
- one 16.5 x 33cm (6½ x 13in) fan print bag
front • one 9.5 x 33cm (3¾ x 13in) fan print
bag back • one patchwork strip • one 9.5 x
33cm (3¾ x 13in) fan print bag back • 11.5
x 33cm (4½ x 13in) fan print top flap • one
patchwork strip 5 x 33cm (2 x 13in) • fan
print bottom flap (**B**). Press seams in
one direction.

(B)

3. Iron the 33 x 54.5cm (13 x 21½in) rectangle of fusible interfacing to the wrong side of the outer bag completed in step 2.

4. To shape the flap corners, on two corners of the outer bag where the fan print bottom flap is positioned measure 4cm (1½in) up from the corner in each direction. Mark with a marking pencil and then cut along the diagonal cutting off each corner (**C**).

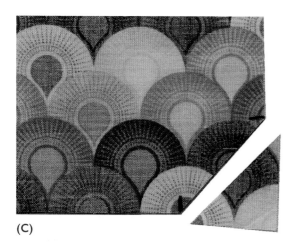

(C)

5. Add one half of the magnetic snap to the centre on the outside of the outer bag, positioning the snap 7cm (2¾in) from the lower edge of the bag front. This is the opposite end to the cut corners.

TO STITCH THE LINING:
6. Iron the 31.5 x 56cm (12½ x 21in) rectangle of fusible wadding (batting) to the wrong side of the 33 x 54.5cm (13 x 21½ in) rectangle of green spot lining.

7. Quilt diagonal lines of varying widths apart over the lining (**D**).

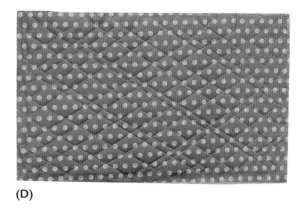

(D)

8. Shape the corners of one end of the lining by following the instructions in step 4.

9. Add the remaining half of the magnetic snap to the centre on the right side of the lining (the end with the cut corners) positioning the snap 4cm (1½in) up from the bottom edge (**E**).

(E)

TO STITCH THE BAG TOGETHER:

10. Lay the lining on top of the outer bag, right sides together. Stitch the 33cm (13in) ends together so that you are stitching the lining to the fan print bag front. Do not stitch the shaped ends.

11. Keeping the layers of lining and outer bag on top of each other, measure 15cm (6in) up from the stitched edge. Fold this inside on itself so that it forms an inner folded pouch. There will now be four layers of fabric on top of each other for 15cm (6in) and the quilted wadding (batting) will be right side facing the interfacing.

12. Carefully pin the lining to the outer bag around the outer edge, making sure that the 15cm (6in) inner pouch is secure. Stitch around the outer edge, leaving a 7.5cm (3in) opening along one side.

13. Clip the diagonal seams and corners. Turn the bag right sides out through the opening and stitch closed. Topstitch around the flap of the bag.

HANDY HINTS:

• Give the seams and the outer edges of the clutch a press with the iron before stitching the opening closed. This will give the bag a crisp finish.

• Replace the red plain fabric in the patchwork with a luxurious silk fabric or a textured fabric for an alternative look.

Pleated Day Bag

A casual bag for going out and about.

A casual bag for going out and about.

Size: 28 × 35.5 × 10cm (11 × 14 × 4in) excluding handles

SKILL LEVEL: EASY

A fun casual bag for those essential bits and pieces we all carry around. I have used a cute owl print for the main body of the bag but any funky print would work well. The contrasting pink and lime green fabrics for the patchwork add zing while the additional pleats at the top give the bag a little extra room. The addition of a small owl charm made from leftover fabric scraps personalises the bag a little more.

MATERIALS

FABRIC
- 50cm (20in) owl print fabric for outer bag and charm
- 50cm (20in) pink floral fabric for the patchwork and lining
- 30cm (12in) green print for the patchwork and handles
- 10cm (4in) square green felt for the charm
- 5cm (2in) pink dot fabric for the patchwork

WADDING (BATTING)/INTERFACING
- 50 cm (20in) fusible wadding
- 7.5cm (3in) firm fusible interfacing

HABERDASHERY
- 10cm (4in) square fusible webbing
- one magnetic snap

CUTTING

All cutting instructions include a 0.75cm (¼in) seam allowance.

Owl print fabric

- four 13.5 x 35.5cm (5¼ x 14in) rectangles for the outer bag
- four 7.5 x 29cm (3 x 11½in) strips for the top band and facing
- one 3 x 18cm (1¼ x 7in) strip for the charm

Pink floral fabric

- two 35.5 x 37cm (14 x 14½in) rectangles for the lining
- eight 5cm (2in) squares for the patchwork

Green print fabric

- two 10 x 81.5cm (4 x 32in) strips for the handles
- ten 5 x 13cm (2 x 5in) rectangles for the patchwork

Pink dot fabric

- sixteen 5cm (2in) squares for the patchwork

Fusible wadding (batting)

- two 35.5 x 37cm (14 x 14½in) rectangles for the lining
- two 6.5 x 28cm (2½ x 11in) strips for the top band
- two 4.5 x 81.5cm (1¾ x 32in) strips for the handles

Firm fusible interfacing

- two 6.5 x 28cm (2½ x 11in) strips for the top band facing

STEP BY STEP

TO STITCH THE PATCHWORK:

1. Stitch a 5cm (2in) pink dot square to each side of a 5cm (2in) pink floral square (**A**). Press seams away from the centre square. Stitch eight of these units.

(A)

2. Take five 5 x 13cm (2 x 5in) green print rectangles and four of the units completed in step 1 and stitch together vertically, beginning with a rectangle and alternating with a pieced unit (**B**).

Press seams towards the rectangles. Repeat with the remaining rectangles and units from step 1. You now have two patchwork pieces.

(B)

TO STITCH THE OUTER BAG:

3. Take the four 13.5 × 35.5cm (5¼ × 14in) owl print rectangles and stitch one to the top and bottom of each patchwork (**C**). Press seams towards the owl print. These will form the outer bag.

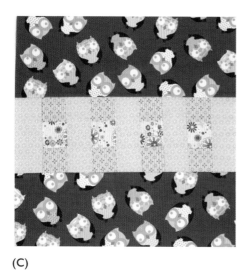

(C)

4. Iron a 35.5 × 37cm (14 × 14½in) rectangle of fusible wadding (batting) to the wrong side of each outer bag piece.

5. Quilt each outer bag piece in straight lines from top to bottom, stitching lines 1.5cm (½in) apart.

6. Mark the centre at the top of each outer piece and fold a small pleat on each side of the mark. Pin and tack (baste) in place. The top edge should now measure 29cm (11½in).

7. Take two 7.5 × 29cm (3 × 11½in) owl print strips for the top band and iron a 6.5 × 28cm (2½ × 11in) strip of fusible wadding (batting) to the wrong side of each. The wadding should be 0.75cm (¼in) less than the band on each edge. Quilt each top band in straight lines horizontally, stitching lines 1.5cm (½in) apart.

TO STITCH THE OWL CHARM AND ADD THE TOP BAND:

8. Select a motif from the leftover owl print fabric. Iron the motif to the wrong side of the fusible webbing. Cut out and remove the backing paper. Iron the motif onto half of the green felt and cut out, leaving a 0.75cm (¼in) of felt showing around the edge.

9. To make the charm string take the 3 × 18cm (1¼ × 7in) owl print strip and press under 0.75cm (¼in) on each long edge. Fold the strip so that the folded edges meet and the right side of the fabric is facing outwards. Topstitch along the folded edge.

10. Using the remaining green felt, position the charm string between the cut out owl motif and the second piece of felt. Stitch around the edge of the owl motif, ensuring that the string is securely attached with the stitching (**D**). Cut around the owl motif, taking care not to cut the string.

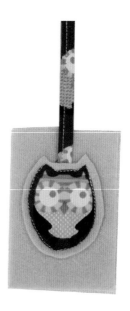

(D)

11. Pin the charm string to the top edge of one outer bag section, 6.5cm (2½in) in from the outer edge. Tack (baste) in place.

12. Stitch a quilted top band as completed in step 7 to the top of each outer bag (**E**). Press seams.

(E)

TO STITCH THE LINING:

13. Take the remaining two 7.5 × 29cm (3 × 11½in) owl print strips for the top band facing and iron a 6.5 × 28cm (2½ × 11in) strip of fusible interfacing to each. The interfacing should be 0.75cm (¼in) less than the band on each edge.

14. Take the two 35.5 × 37cm (14 × 14½in) pink floral rectangles for the lining and mark the centre at the top on each 35.5cm (14in) side. Fold a small pleat on each side of the mark. Pin and then tack (baste) in place. The top edge should now measure 29cm (11½in).

15. Stitch a top band facing as completed in step 13 to the top of each lining piece (**F**). Press seams. You now have two lining pieces.

(F)

16. Add a magnetic snap to the centre of each top band facing, positioning the snap approximately 2.5cm (1in) from the top edge with the fabric right side facing.

TO STITCH THE HANDLES:

17. Take the two 10 × 81.5cm (4 × 32in) green print strips and press under 0.75cm (¼in) on one long edge.

18. Lay a 4.5 × 81.5cm (1¾ × 32in) strip of fusible wadding (batting) down the centre of the wrong side of each green print strip. Iron in place.

19. Fold the raw edge of the fabric to the centre of the wadding (batting), and then the folded edge on top. The folded edge should overlap the raw edge by 0.75cm (¼in) Pin in place. Topstitch the folded edge. Stitch 0.75cm (¼in) in from each outer edge on both handles.

TO STITCH THE BAG TOGETHER:

20. Pin the ends of the handles to the top edge of each outer bag band (**G**). Position them in 5cm (2in) from the outer edges. Tack (baste) in place.

(G)

21. Place an outer bag on top of a lining piece, right sides together, and stitch across the top band. Press the seam open. Repeat with the second outer bag and lining.

22. Lay both pieces completed in step 21 on top of each other, right sides together, so that the outer bag pieces are matching each other and the lining pieces are matching each other. Pin around the edge ensuring that the patchwork, the top and lining match up. Leave a 13cm (5in) opening in the centre bottom of the lining. Stitch around the edge, making sure that the handles and charm are not caught in the stitching as you sew.

23. To shape the base of the bag match the base seam with the side seam. Measure in 2½in (6.5cm) along the seam line and stitch across. Cut off the excess fabric. Repeat for all four corners (**H**).

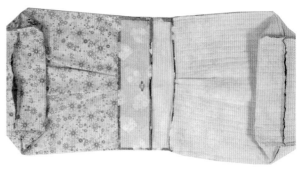

(H)

24. To finish, turn the bag through the opening and stitch the opening in the lining closed. Topstitch around the top edge of the bag and the bottom edge of the band.

HANDY HINTS:

• If using a directional fabric ensure that the fabric is cut and positioned correctly when stitching the outer bag pieces.

• When making the bag charm, if your fabric does not have an identifiable motif, cut a 5cm (2in) circle of fabric and use this instead. It is just as effective.

Simply Delicious Lunch Bag

A pretty and practical lunch bag.

A pretty and practical lunch bag.

Size: 7½in × 9in × 4½in (19cm × 23cm × 11.5cm) excluding handle

SKILL LEVEL: REQUIRES EXPERIENCE

Banish the midday blues with this stylish lunch bag. The fresh fabric choices and compact construction make this bag ideal for everyday use. The inside is lined with plastic so that the lovely fabric is protected and the inside of the bag can be wiped clean after use. No one else will have a lunch bag quite like this!

MATERIALS

FABRIC
- 75cm (30in) green stripe fabric for the back, flap and lining
- 50cm (20in) pink spot fabric for the binding
- 35.5cm (14in) house print fabric for the side panels
- 25.5cm (10in) flower print fabric for the front panel and handle pad

WADDING (BATTING)/INTERFACING
- 38cm (15in) fusible wadding
- 50cm (20in) Vilene lamifix (Pellon lamifix) or similar for the protective lining

HABERDASHERY
- 63.5 × 2.5cm (25 × 1in) wide pink cotton webbing for the handle
- 10cm (4in) strip hook and loop fastening
- 6.5cm (2½in) diameter circle template

CUTTING

All cutting instructions include a 0.75cm (¼in) seam allowance.

Green stripe fabric

- two 19 x 35.5cm (7½ x 14in) rectangles for the back flap and lining for the back flap
- one 19 x 23cm (7½ x 9in) rectangle for the lining
- one 13 x 63.5cm (5 x 25in) rectangle for the lining

Pink spot fabric

- one 4 x 188cm (½in x 74in) strip cut on the bias for the binding (smaller strips can be stitched together to make this)

House print fabric

- one 13 x 63.5cm (5 x 25in) rectangle for the side panels and bottom. If your fabric is a one way design you will need to cut two 13 x 33cm (5 x 13in) rectangles instead of one long rectangle.

Flower print fabric

- one 19 x 23cm (7½ x 9in) rectangle for the front panel
- one 11.5cm (4½in) square for the handle pad

Vilene lamifix or similar

- one 19 x 35.5cm (7½ x 14in) rectangle for the lining
- one 19 x 23cm (7½ x 9in) rectangle for the lining
- one 13 x 63.5cm (5 x 25in) rectangle for the lining

Fusible wadding (batting)

- one 18 x 34.5cm (7 x 13½in) rectangle for the back flap
- one 18 x 22cm (7 x 8½in) rectangle for the front panel
- one 11.5 x 62.5cm (4½ x 24½in) rectangle for the side panels and bottom
- one 11.5cm (4½in) square for the handle

STEP BY STEP

THE PROTECTIVE LINING:

1. Following the manufacturer's instructions, iron the Vilene lamifix to the right side of each corresponding piece of green striped lining fabric. Leave to cool.

TO STITCH THE OUTER BAG:

2. Iron the fusible wadding (batting) to each corresponding piece of outer bag fabric.

3. If you have cut your house print fabric into two rectangles because you have directional fabric, stitch the rectangles together to make a 63.5cm (25in) strip. The direction of the pattern on the fabric will need to face away from the centre seam in opposite directions.

4. Take the 13 x 63.5cm (5 x 25in) rectangle of house print fabric and lay this in front of you horizontally. Place the 19 x 35.5cm (7½ x 14in) green rectangle above it and the 19 x 23cm (7½ x 9in) flower print rectangle below it. Measure in 22.5cm (8¾in) from the outer edge of the house print rectangle and pin one 19cm (7½in) side of each of the fabric pieces to it. Stitch across leaving 0.75cm (¼in) free at each end (**A**). Press seams away from the centre.

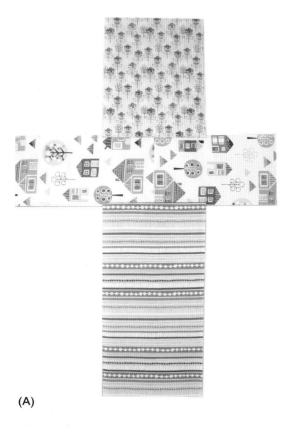

(A)

5. Separate the strip of hook and loop fastening into two pieces. Measure 5cm (2in) down from the top of the flower print front panel and, with right sides facing, stitch one piece of hook and loop fasteing to the front of the bag, stitching around all four edges.

TO STITCH THE LINING:

6. Repeat step 4 but with the green striped lining pieces, taking care when pressing the seams not to damage the lamifix.

7. To add the hook and loop fastening to the lining measure down 4cm (1½in) from the top edge of the 19 x 35.5cm (7½ x 14in) back flap piece and, with right sides facing, stitch the fastening to the lining.

TO STITCH THE BAG TOGETHER:

8. Lay the lining and the outer bag on top of each other, wrong sides facing, and pin around the outer edges. Place the circle template on each of the two corners of the green striped outer bag flap and mark the curve carefully. Cut around the curve to shape the outer corners.

9. Tack the lining and the outer bag together around all edges.

10. Pin the front section of the bag to each of the side sections (**B**).

(B)

11. Press under 0.75cm (¼in) on one long edge of the bias binding strips. To stitch the binding to one front corner, turn under the short raw edge of the binding. Starting at the base of the corner, stitch the long raw edge of the binding to the raw edges of the front bag corner, stitching through all the layers (**C**). Trim the binding level with the top of the bag front. Roll the folded edge of the binding to the front of the lunch bag and pin in place. Topstitch the binding, stitching through all layers of fabric. Repeat with the other front bag corner.

(C)

12. To stitch the binding to the top inner edge of the bag follow the instructions in step 11 but start stitching the binding to the top edge of one side panel, across the front panel and then to the second side panel. Use just one bias strip. There is no need to turn under the raw edges at the start or end of the binding as they will be covered by the next strip.

13. To stitch the final piece of binding to the sides of the bag at the back and the flap, join the side panels to the back panel and pin in place. Turn under the short raw edge of the binding and starting, at the base of one of the back corners, stitch the binding up the side panel joining the side to the back of the bag, around the flap and down the other side following the instructions in step 11. Before finishing at the bottom corner, turn under the raw edge and stitch in place.

TO STITCH THE HANDLE:

14. To make the handle pad, iron the fusible wadding (batting) to the wrong side of the 11.5cm (4½in) flower print square. Press under 0.75cm (¼in) of fabric on one edge of the fabric square towards the wadding.

15. With right sides facing bring two edges of the square together so that the raw edge is underneath and the folded edge is on top, overlapping by 0.75cm (¼in). Make sure that the folded edge is centred in the middle of the square. Stitch across each end, trim the corners and turn through. Press.

16. To attach the handle pad to the webbing, mark the middle of the webbing and place the handle pad on top. Stitch 0.75cm (¼in) around the pad stitching through the webbing to secure.

17. On each side panel mark 4cm (1½in) down from the top edge. Overlap the webbing by 5cm (2in) from this marking. Turn under 1.5cm (½in) on the raw edge and stitch the webbing down so that the first line of stitching goes across the 4cm (1½in) marking and then goes around in a square, ensuring that the raw edge is stitched down (**D**).

(D)

HANDY HINTS:

• To cut bias strips from fabric, fold the fabric on the diagonal to make a triangle. Cut one 4cm (½in) strip across the diagonal starting at the folded edge.

• I have used a product called Vilene lamifix (Pellon lamifix) to line my bag so that it can be wiped clean. Other products could be substituted here such as thin, clear polythene. Alternatively, the bag could be left unlined and then washed to clean.

Weekend Bag

A super-large roomy bag.

A super-large roomy bag.

Size: 35.5 × 53 × 16.5cm (14 × 20 × 6½in) excluding handles

SKILL LEVEL: REQUIRES EXPERIENCE

This bag is almost like an old-fashioned duffel bag but not quite. It is large and roomy and would be great for a day at the beach or useful for a night away. As the sides are soft and pliable it can be easily stuffed into a small space. There are large pockets on the inside, strong straps on the outside and the bright eye-catching fabric choices make it perfect to brighten up a dull day.

MATERIALS

FABRIC
- 127cm (50in) orange leaf fabric for the patchwork and lining
- 61cm (24in) green print fabric for the bag bottom and drawstrings
- 41cm (16in) red print fabric for the drawstring casing and patchwork
- 25.5cm (10in) green floral print for the patchwork

- 25.5cm (10in) pink print fabric for the patchwork

WADDING (BATTING)
- 1m (40in) fusible wadding

HABERDASHERY
- 3.6m × 2.5cm (144 ×1in) wide red cotton webbing for the handles

CUTTING

All cutting instructions include a ¼in (0.75cm) seam allowance.

Orange leaf fabric
- two 52 × 62.5cm (20½ × 24½in) rectangles for the lining
- two 20.5 × 51cm (8 × 20in) rectangles for the pockets
- ten 11.5cm (4½in) squares for the patchwork

Green print fabric
- two 22 × 52cm (8½ × 20½in) rectangles for the bag bottom
- two 4 × 112cm (1½ × 44in) strips for the drawstrings

Red print fabric
- two 9 × 52cm (3½ × 20½in) strips for the drawstring casing
- ten 11.5cm (4½in) squares for the patchwork

Green floral print fabric
- ten 11.5cm (4½in) squares for the patchwork

Pink print fabric
- ten 11.5cm (4½in) squares for the patchwork

Fusible wadding (batting)
- two 51 × 61cm (20 × 24in) rectangles for the lining

STEP BY STEP

TO STITCH THE PATCHWORK:

1. Take the 11.5cm (4½in) squares and lay them out into two grids of 20 squares – five squares across and four squares down.

2. Stitch the squares together matching the seams (**A**). Press.

(A)

TO STITCH THE OUTER BAG:

3. Stitch a 22 × 52cm (8½ × 20½in) green print rectangle to the bottom of each patchwork unit completed in step 2 (**B**).

(B)

4. Iron a 51 × 61cm (20 × 24in) rectangle of wadding (batting) to the wrong side of the outer bag units completed in step 3.

5. Machine quilt in a grid each of the outer bag pieces, stitching 1cm (½in) away from the seam lines both diagonally and vertically (**C**).

(C)

6. To add the drawstring casing, take the two 9 × 52cm (3½ × 20½in) strips of red print fabric and fold each short end of fabric 0.75cm (¼in) towards the wrong side of the fabric. Repeat again so that the raw edges are enclosed and press. Stitch down.

7. Fold the casing in half lengthways with wrong sides together and press. Centre the casing along the patchwork edge of each outer bag piece with raw edges aligned. The casing will not reach each side of the patchwork but should be centred in the middle with a small gap at each end. Stitch in place (**D**).

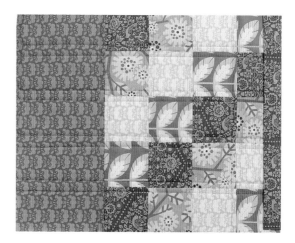

(D)

TO ADD THE HANDLES:

8. Cut the red cotton webbing into two pieces so that each piece measures 182.9cm (72in).

9. Lay a handle on each outer bag piece so that the raw edge of the handle is in line with the bottom of the bag and is placed 14.5cm (5¾in) in from the outer edge, loops up towards the top of the bag to form the handles, and comes down again 14.5cm (5¾in) in from the outer edge. Pin in place. Stitch up each side of the handle stopping at the top of the second patchwork square up from the bottom (**E**). Repeat on the second outer bag piece.

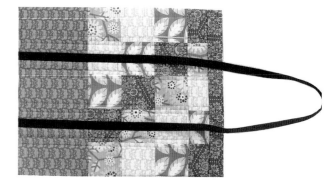

(E)

TO MAKE THE DRAWSTRINGS:

10. Take the two 4 x 112cm (1½ x 44in) green print strips and press under 0.75cm (¼in) along each long edge. Fold the strips in half so that the folded edges are on top of each other and topstitch along the fold (**F**).

(F)

TO STITCH THE LINING:

11. To make the pockets in the lining, fold each 20.5 x 51cm (8 x 20in) orange leaf rectangle in half so that the short sides meet each other. Stitch around the three raw edges leaving a 5cm (2in) gap in the bottom. Clip the corners and turn through.

12. Position each pocket 16.5cm (6½in) from the top of each 52 x 62.5cm (20½ x 24½in) orange leaf lining rectangle and centred equal distance from the raw edges (**G**). Stitch down each side, across the bottom and down the centre to make double pockets.

(G)

13. Place the lining panels together, right sides facing, and stitch down each side and across the bottom, leaving a 15cm (6in) gap in one side for turning. Also leave the top open.

14. To shape the base of the lining, match the base seam with the side seam. Measure in 7.5cm (3in) along the seam line and stitch across. Cut off the excess fabric. Repeat on the other corner.

TO STITCH THE BAG TOGETHER:

15. Place the outer bag panels together, right sides facing, and stitch down each side and across the bottom, making sure that the patchwork matches on the side seams.

16. To shape the base of the outer bag, match the base seam with the side seam. Measure in 7.5cm (3in) along the seam line and stitch across. Double stitch across the stitching for added strength. Cut off the excess fabric. Repeat on the other corner.

17. Keeping the bag right side out and the lining right side in, place the outer bag inside the lining.

18. Matching the side seams and keeping the casing and handles pushed down inside the bag, stitch around the top edge of the bag.

19. Turn the bag through the opening and stitch the opening in the lining closed. Carefully press the top of the bag so that the lining lays flat. Topstitch around the edge of the bag (not the casing).

20. Starting on the right side, thread one drawstring through the front casing, back through the back casing and tie the ends in a knot at the right side. Repeat the process with the second drawstring but start on the left side. Attaching a safety pin to one end of the drawstring will help to thread it through.

HANDY HINTS:

• If you want to make this bag more quickly, buy cord for the drawstrings instead of making them from fabric.

• The patchwork outer bag could be made entirely from fabric scraps or even recycled or pre-loved fabrics to achieve a scrappy patchwork look.

Spotty Dotty Messenger Bag

A big bag for work or play.

A big bag for work or play.

Size: 30 × 30 × 7.5cm (12 × 12 × 3in) excluding handles

SKILL LEVEL: EASY

A smart medium-sized messenger bag, big enough for holding a book, papers, pens and pencils as well as all those other essentials! The buckle trim on the front of the flap is for decoration only but gives the bag that professional-looking finish while showcasing the bold fabric design. The cream dotty fabric used for the lining compliments the outer fabric and is seen every time the flap is opened.

MATERIALS

FABRIC
- 101.5cm (40in) green spot fabric for the outer bag, flap, pocket and strap loops
- 75cm (30in) cream spot for the inner bag, flap and patchwork strap
- 15cm (6in) green stripe fabric for the long strap and patchwork strap

WADDING (BATTING)/INTERFACING
- 2.5cm (1in) fusible wadding
- 75cm (30in) firm fusible interfacing

HABERDASHERY
- 2.5cm (1in) rectangular metal buckle
- two 2.5cm (1in) rectangular metal rings for the strap loops
- 20.5cm (8in) diameter circle template

CUTTING

All cutting instructions include a 0.75cm (¼in) seam allowance.

Green spot fabric

- one 35.3 × 63.5cm (14 × 25in) rectangle for the outer bag
- one 30 × 13cm (12 × 5in) strip for the upper flap
- one 30 × 11.5cm (12 × 4½in) strip for the lower flap
- two 23 × 14cm (9 × 5½in) rectangles for the inner pocket
- two 6.5 × 13cm (2½ × 5in) strips for the strap loops

Cream spot fabric

- one 35.3 × 63.5cm (14 × 25in) rectangle for the bag lining
- one 30 × 9cm (12 × 3½in) strip for the mid flap
- one 30cm (12in) square for flap lining
- four 4cm (1½in) squares for the patchwork

Green stripe fabric

- one 6.5 × 112cm (2½ × 44in) strip for the long strap
- five 4cm (1½in) squares for the patchwork
- one 4 × 24cm (1½ × 9½in) strip for the patchwork lining

Fusible interfacing

- one 35.3 × 63.5cm (14 × 25in) rectangle for the outer bag
- one 30cm (12in) square for the flap

Fusible wadding (batting)

- one 2.5 × 112cm (1 × 44in) for strap

STEP BY STEP

TO STITCH THE FLAP:

1. Take the 30 × 9cm (12 × 3½in) cream spot strip and stitch the 30 × 13cm (12 × 5in) green spot strip to the top and the 30 × 11.5cm (12 × 4½in) green spot strip to the bottom, joining the long edges. Press the seams towards the dark fabric.

2. Iron the 30cm (12in) square of fusible interfacing to the wrong side of the unit completed in step 1. You now have one outer flap.

3. Place a 20.5cm (8in) diameter circle template onto one bottom corner of the outer flap so that the edges of the template touch both the side and the bottom of the flap. Mark the curve. Repeat on the other corner. Cut along each curve (**A**).

(A)

4. Repeat step 3 with the cream spot flap lining.

TO STITCH THE PATCHWORK STRAP:

5. Stitch the nine 1½in (4cm) striped and cream spot squares in a row starting with a striped square and alternating the squares. Press seams all one way.

6. Lay the patchwork right sides together onto the 4 × 24cm (1½ × 9½in) striped strip. Stitch down both long sides and across the bottom, gently curving the corners. Trim corners and clip curves. Turn right side out. Press.

TO COMPLETE THE FLAP:

7. Place the outer flap and the lining flap right sides together. Stitch all the way around leaving a 10cm (4in) gap in the middle of the top edge, backstitching at the beginning and end. Clip corners and curves. Turn right side out and press. Topstitch all the way around the edge.

8. Mark the centre of the top edge of the flap and lay the patchwork strap down the middle, turning the raw ends of the strap underneath itself. Topstitch around the outer edge of the patchwork strap, stitching 14cm (5½in) down each side, across the middle and the top so that half of the strap is secured to the flap. Slide the buckle onto the unstitched part of the strap as far as it will go and then stitch across the strap as close to the buckle as possible, securing it to the flap. The remainder of the patchwork strap will be unsecured (**B**).

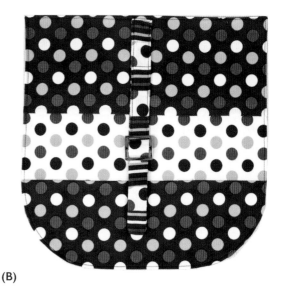

(B)

TO STITCH THE LINING:

9. Take the two 23 × 14cm (9 × 5½in) green spot rectangles for the inner pocket and place them right sides together. Stitch around the edge leaving a 5cm (2in) opening on one long side. Clip corners, turn right side out and press.

10. Take the 35.3 × 63.5cm (14 × 25in) cream spot rectangle for the lining and position the pocket 10cm (4in) from the top on the right side of the fabric. Topstitch around three edges, leaving the top open. Stitch down the centre from top to bottom to make two small pockets (**C**).

11. Fold the lining piece in half, right sides together, and stitch down each side.

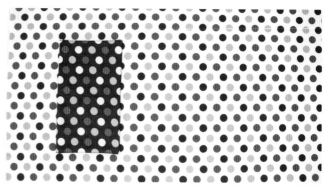

(C)

TO STITCH THE STRAP AND STRAP LOOPS:

12. Take the 6.5 x 112cm (2½ x 44in) strip of striped fabric and press under 0.75cm (¼in) on one long edge. Lay the 2.5 x 112cm (1 x 44in) strip of fusible wadding down the centre of the wrong side of the strap. Iron in place.

13. Fold the raw edge of the fabric to the centre of the wadding and then the folded edge on top. The folded edge should overlap the raw edge by 0.75cm (¼in) Pin in place. Top stitch the folded edge. Top stitch each outer edge (**D**).

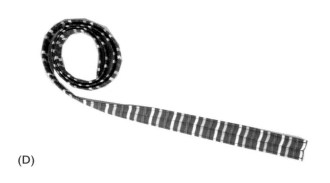

(D)

14. To stitch the strap loops, take the two 6.5 x 13cm (2½ x 5in) strips of green spot fabric and press under 0.75cm (¼in) on each long edge. Fold in half so that the right side of the fabric is facing out and topstitch down the folded edge. Topstitch down the opposite edge, also.

15. Insert each strap loop into a rectangular ring. Fold the loop in half and make sure that the raw edges are even. Stitch across the fabric 0.75cm (¼in) away from the ring (**E**).

(E)

TO STITCH THE OUTER BAG:

16. Iron the 35. x 63.5cm (14 x 25in) rectangle of fusible interfacing onto the wrong side of the 35.3 x 63.5cm (14in x 25in) green spot for the outer bag.

17. Lay the flap right side up on the right side of the outer bag positioning the flap 4cm (1½in) from the top edge. Stitch across the flap, securing the flap to the outer bag over the top of your previous stitches. Stitch across the flap again 0.75cm (¼in) below this first line of stitching for extra reinforcement (**F**).

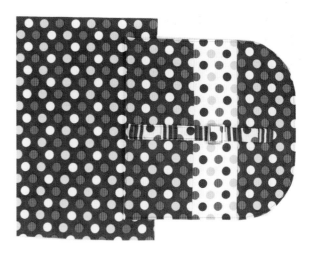

(F)

18. Fold the outer bag in half, right sides together, tucking the flap down inside, out of the way. Stitch down both sides.

19. To shape the base of the bag, match the centre fold of the base with the side seam. Measure in 4cm (1½in) along the seam line and stitch across. Cut off the excess fabric. Repeat on the other corner and again on the two lining corners.

TO STITCH THE BAG TOGETHER:

20. Turn the outer bag right side out. Pin a strap loop to each side, making sure that the strap is centred over the side seam and that the raw edges are even with the top of the bag. Tack (baste) in place.

21. Put the outer bag inside the lining so that the right sides are facing. Make sure that the pocket on the lining is on the same side of the bag as the flap. The flap and strap loops are pushed down between the two layers. Pin the outer bag and the lining together at the top, lining up the side seams and the raw edges.

22. Stitch around the top edge, double stitching over the strap loops for reinforcement and leaving a 13cm (5in) opening in the centre of the flap side for turning. Back stitch at the beginning and end.

23. Turn the bag through the opening and press the seam around the top edge of the bag so that it lays flat. Press under the seam allowance on the opening and then topstitch all the way around the top of the bag.

24. Thread the strap through the rings on the strap loops. Turn under the raw edge on the strap and topstitch it to itself 2.5cm (1in) up from the ring. Stitch across the strap several times for extra strength.

HANDY HINTS:

• When you have turned the bag through, before topstitching the top edge, if possible press the seams to give the bag a neat, crisp finish.

• I haven't added a magnetic fastening to the flap of this bag as the flap extends a considerable way over the bag, but if you wished to you would need to add the fastening at the end of step 6 to the inside of the flap and at the end of step 20 to the outer bag.

Super-Sized Satchel

A softly padded super-sized satchel.

A softly padded super-sized satchel.

Size: 38 × 25.5 × 7.5cm (15 × 10 × 3in) excluding strap

SKILL LEVEL: REQUIRES EXPERIENCE

A large satchel suitable for the office, school or college. Roomy enough to carry a laptop, books and stationery and softly padded to protect the contents. The fabric choice here lends itself to the world of work and the modern geometric print and lettering is right on trend. The pockets both inside and out ensure that there is plenty of storage for all those work essentials.

MATERIALS

FABRIC
- 89cm (35in) white print fabric for the lining, outer bag side and bottom panels, inner pockets, patchwork, strap and strap loops
- 75cm (30in) brown print fabric for the outer bag, outer pockets, outer flap and strap
- 20.5cm (8in) plain black fabric for the patchwork and outer pocket trim

WADDING (BATTING)/INTERFACING
- 38cm (15in) fusible wadding
- 35.5cm (14in) firm fusible interfacing

HABERDASHERY
- two 4cm (1½in) metal D rings
- one 4cm (½in) buckle
- 8in (20.5cm) diameter circle template

CUTTING

All cutting instructions include a 0.75cm (¼in) seam allowance.

White print fabric
- two 27 × 39.5cm (10½ × 15½in) rectangles for the lining
- one 27 × 39.5cm (10½ × 15½in) rectangle for the flap lining
- two 16.5 × 39.5cm (6½ × 15½in) rectangles for the inner pockets
- two 9 × 39.5cm (3½ × 15½in) strips for the outer and inner bottom panels
- four 9 × 27cm (3½ × 10½in) strips for outer and inner side panels
- one 5 × 107cm (2 × 42in) strip for the strap
- one 6.5 × 11.5cm (2½ × 4½in) rectangle for the patchwork on the flap
- two 6.5 × 11.5cm (2 × 4½in) rectangles for the strap loops

Brown print fabric
- one 27 × 39.5cm (10½ × 15½in) rectangles for the outer bag
- two 13 × 27cm (5 × 10½in) rectangles for the flap
- four 4 × 16.5cm (1½ × 6½in) strips for the patchwork on the flap
- two 13 × 39.5cm (5 × 15½in) rectangles for the outer pockets
- one 5 × 107cm (2 × 42in) strip for the strap

Black fabric
- one 15 × 39.5cm (6 × 15½in) rectangle for the outer pocket trim
- four 4 × 16.5cm (1½ × 6½in) strips for the patchwork on the flap

- two 4 × 11.5cm (1½ × 2½in) strips for the patchwork on the flap

Fusible wadding (batting)
- two 24 × 37cm (9½ × 14½in) rectangles for the outer bag
- one 6.5 × 37cm (2½ × 14½in) strip for the outer bottom panel
- two 6.5 × 24cm (2½ × 9½in) strips for the outer side panels

Firm fusible interfacing
- one 27 × 39.5cm (10½ × 15½in) rectangle for the flap lining
- one 18 × 39.5cm (7 × 15½in) rectangle for the outer pocket lining
- one 4 × 107cm (1½ × 42in) strip for the strap

STEP BY STEP

TO STITCH THE PATCHWORK:

1. Stitch a black 4 × 11.5cm (1½ × 2½in) strip to each side of the 6.5 × 11.5cm (2½ × 4½in) white print rectangle. Press seams away from the centre.

2. Take the four 4 × 16.5cm (1½ × 6½in) black strips and the four 4 × 16.5cm (1½ × 6½in) brown strips and stitch together, alternating the strips, into two units with four strips in each unit. Start with a brown print strip when stitching each unit. Press seams downwards.

3. Stitch the units made in step 2 to each side of the unit made in step 1 ensuring that a black strip is stitched to the white print rectangle.

4. Stitch a 13 x 27cm (5 x 10½in) brown rectangle to each side of the patchwork unit (**A**).

(A)

TO STITCH THE FLAP:

5. Iron the 27 x 39.5cm (10½ x 15½in) rectangle of interfacing to the wrong side of the patchwork.

6. With right sides together, place the patchwork on top of the 27 x 39.5cm (10½ x 15½in) white print rectangle. Stitch down each side and across the bottom, leaving the top open. Trim the corners and turn right side out.

7. Topstitch 0.75cm (¼in) away from the folded edges. Topstitch 0.75cm (¼in) away from the centre patchwork rectangle. The flap is now completed.

TO STITCH THE LINING:

8. To make the inner pocket, take the two 16.5 x 39.5cm (6½ x 15½in) white print rectangles and, with right sides facing, stitch together along the long edges. Turn through, press and topstitch along the top edge.

9. Lay the pocket on top of one of the 27 x 39.5cm (10½ x 15½ in) white print lining rectangles. Position the pocket 9cm (3½in) from the top of the lining fabric. Stitch along the bottom edge. Stitch vertically down the centre of the pocket to create two pocket compartments.

10. Stitch a 9 x 39.5cm (3½ x 15½in) white print bottom panel to the bottom of the unit completed in step 9. Start and stop stitching 0.75cm (¼in) from each end.

11. Flip this bottom panel down and stitch a 9 x 27cm (3½ x 10½in) white print side panel to each side. Stop stitching 0.75cm (¼in) from the bottom of each strip (**B**).

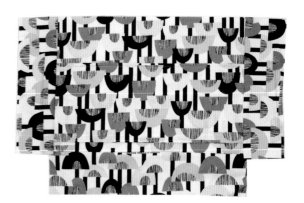

(B)

12. Align the corners and stitch to join the side panels to the bottom panel.

13. Stitch the remaining 27 × 39.5cm (10½ × 15½in) white print lining rectangle to the unit made in step 12. Stitch the side seams first and then stitch across the bottom leaving a 15cm (6in) opening.

TO STITCH THE OUTER BAG:
14. To make the outer pocket, stitch a 13 × 39.5cm (5 × 15½in) brown print rectangle to each side of the 15 × 39.5cm (6 × 15½in) black strip. Press seams towards the black strip.

15. Iron a 18 × 39.5cm (7 × 15½in) strip of interfacing to the reverse of one half of the pocket. Fold the pocket in half so that the black strip is at the top and the right side of the fabric is facing outwards. Topstitch across the top edge.

16. Take the two 27 × 39.5cm (10½ × 15½in) brown print outer bag rectangles, one 9 × 39.5cm (3½ × 15½in) white print outer bag bottom panel, and two 9 × 27cm (3½ × 10½in) white print outer bag side panels and iron the corresponding fusible webbing to each piece.

17. Quilt each of the outer bag pieces in a grid, quilting 7.5cm (3in) apart vertically and 5cm (2in) apart horizontally (**C**).

(C)

18. Quilt the side and bottom panels with rows of stitching 5cm (2in) apart (**D**).

(D)

19. Lay the pocket completed in step 15 on top of one of the quilted outer bag pieces, aligning the bottom edges. Tack (baste) in place. Stitch vertically down the centre of the pocket to create two pocket compartments (**E**).

(E)

20. Stitch together the outer bag in the same way that you have stitched the lining in steps 10 to 13, but you do not need to leave an opening in the bottom. Turn the bag through.

TO STITCH THE STRAP LOOPS AND STRAP:

21. To stitch the strap loops, take the two 6.5 × 11.5cm (2 × 4½in) white print rectangles and fold each in half lengthwise and stitch. Turn through, press and topstitch down each side.

22. Insert each strap loop into a D ring. Fold the loop in half and make sure that the raw edges are aligned. Stitch across the fabric 0.75cm (¼in) away from the ring (**F**).

(F)

23. To stitch the strap, take the 5 × 107cm (2 × 42in) white print strip and iron the 4 × 107cm (1½ × 42in) strip of interfacing to the reverse. Stitch the 5 × 107cm (2 × 42in) brown print strip to one long edge. Fold under 0.75cm (¼in) on the remaining two raw edges and bring these together so that they lie on top of each other. Topstitch down each long edge (**G**).

(G)

TO STITCH THE BAG TOGETHER:

24. Pin the flap, right sides facing, to the outer bag. The flap should be on top of the outer pockets with the raw edges aligned. Stitch across with a 0.3cm (1/8in) seam.

25. Pin a strap loop to each side panel, making sure that the loop is centred over the panel and that the raw edges are aligned with the top of the bag. Stitch in place using a double row of stitching.

26. Place the outer bag inside the lining so that the right sides are facing and the inner pockets are on the same side as the flap. Make sure that the flap and the strap loops are tucked down inside the bag. Matching the side seams, stitch around the top of the bag to join the lining and the bag together.

27. Turn the bag right side out through the opening left in the lining. Stitch the opening closed.

28. Press gently and then topstitch 0.75cm (¼in) all the way around the top edge of the bag to create a neat finish.

29. To add the strap, thread one end through one of the D rings on a strap loop. Fold under the raw edge and stitch it back on itself with a double row of stitching. Slide the buckle onto the other end of the strap and then thread the remaining strap through the D ring and then through the underneath side of the buckle, bringing it back on itself and stitching in place.

Gathered Top
Tulip Bag

A very sweet little day bag.

A very sweet little day bag.

Size: 28 × 25.5 × 7.5cm (11 × 10 × 3in) excluding handles

SKILL LEVEL: REQUIRES EXPERIENCE

A bright and very cute bag which reminds me of tulips in spring time. Whenever I look at this bag it always makes me smile with its colourful fabric and fun design. The additional pockets on the front and back provide extra storage and the gathered top makes the bag surprisingly roomy.

MATERIALS

FABRIC
- 50cm (20in) white print fabric for the outer bag
- 56cm (22in) green print for the lining, pocket lining and patchwork squares
- 35.5cm (14in) pink print for the handles, casings and drawstrings
- 7.5cm (3in) pink stripe for the patchwork squares

INTERFACING
- 50cm (20in) firm fusible interfacing

CUTTING

All cutting instructions include a 0.75cm (¼in) seam allowance.

White print fabric
- two 33 x 33cm (13 x 13in) squares for the outer bag
- two 10 x 33cm (4 x 13in) strips for the lower outer bag

Green print fabric
- two 33 x 33cm (13 x 13in) squares for the lining
- two 16.5 x 33cm (6½ x 13in) strips for the lining for the lower outer bag
- nine 5cm (2in) squares for the patchwork

Pink print fabric
- two 7.5 x 81.5cm (3 x 32in) strips for the handles
- two 6.5 x 24cm (2½ x 9½in) strips for the casings
- two 4 x 81.5cm (1½ x 32in) strips for the drawstrings

Pink stripe fabric
- nine 5cm (2in) squares for the patchwork

Firm fusible interfacing
- two 33 x 33cm (13 x 13in) squares for the outer bag
- two 14 x 33cm (5½ x 13in) strips for the lower outer bag

STEP BY STEP

TO STITCH THE PATCHWORK:

1. Take nine 5cm (2in) green print squares and nine 5cm (2in) pink strip squares and stitch together into two rows of nine, alternating the fabrics. Press seams in one direction. Trim 1.7cm (⅝in) from the end of each row so that the rows measure 33cm (13in). You now have two patchwork pieces (**A**).

(A)

TO STITCH THE LOWER OUTER BAG:

2. Stitch each patchwork piece to a 10 x 33cm (4 x 13in) white print strip (**B**). Press seams towards the patchwork. Iron a 14 x 33cm (5½ x 13in) strip of fusible interfacing to the wrong side of each lower outer bag piece.

(B)

3. Stitch a 16.5 x 33cm (6½ x 13in) green print strip of lining fabric to the patchwork edge of each of the two units completed in step 2. Open out and press seam towards the lining. Fold the lining so that the wrong side of the lining is facing the wrong side of the lower outer bag piece. Align the bottom edges together and press. This should give 1.5cm (½in) of lining fabric showing above the patchwork squares on the top edge of the lower outer bag. Tack (baste) the bottom edges together. Topstitch the top edge.

TO STITCH THE LINING:

4. Take the the two 33 x 33cm (13 x 13in) green print lining squares and place them on top of each other, right sides facing. Stitch down each side and across the bottom leaving a 10cm (4in) opening in one side for turning.

5. To shape the base of the lining, match the centre fold of the base with the side seam. Measure in 4cm (1½in) along the seam line (**C**) and stitch across. Cut off the excess fabric. Repeat on the other corner.

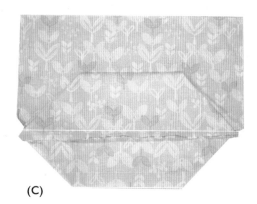

(C)

TO STITCH THE HANDLES:

6. Fold each 7.5 x 81.5cm (3 x 32in) pink print strip in half, right sides facing, and stitch down each long edge to form a tube.

Turn right side out and press so that the seam line is along one edge. You now have the two handles.

7. Iron a 33 x 33cm (13 x 13in) square of fusible interfacing to the reverse of each 33 x 33cm (13 x 13in) square of white print outer bag fabric.

8. Place each outer bag panel right side up and place a lower outer bag panel on top, right side up, ensuring that the bottom edges align. Tack (baste) in place.

9. Measure in 6.5cm (2½in) from each side of the bottom edge and place the raw ends of each handle in line with the edge. Stitch the handle in place through both the lower outer bag and also through the outer bag. Stitch up one side of the handle, across the top of the handle where it meets the top edge of the lower outer bag twice, and down to the bottom (**D**). Repeat this for each handle end.

(D)

10. Take the two 6.5 × 24cm (2½ × 9½in) pink print strips for the casings and fold each in half, right sides facing. Stitch along the length, leaving a 5cm (2in) gap in the centre for turning. Press seams so that they sit in the middle of the casing and then stitch across each short end. Turn through and press.

11. Position each casing 5cm (2in) from the top of each outer bag panel and centred in the middle of the panel. Topstitch each casing strip to the outer bag across the top and bottom. Leave the ends open and ensure the handles are out of the way.

12. Place the outer bag panels together, right sides facing, and stitch down each side and across the bottom, leaving the top open. The lower outer bag and handles will now be stitched in place.

13. To shape the base of the bag, match the centre fold of the base with the side seam. Measure in 4cm (1½in) along the seam line and stitch across. Cut off the excess fabric. Repeat on the other corner. Turn the bag right side out (**E**).

(E)

14. Keeping the bag right side out and the lining right side in, place the outer bag inside the lining (**F**).

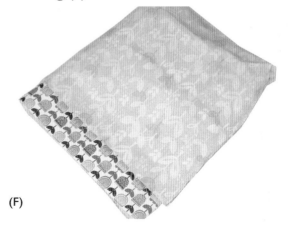

(F)

15. Matching the side seams and keeping the handles firmly stuffed down, stitch around the top edge of the bag.

16. Turn the bag right side out through the opening and stitch the opening in the lining closed. Carefully press the top of the bag so that the lining is 0.75 cm (¼in) above the top edge of the outer bag. Topstitch around the edge and also in the seam line where the lining meets the outer bag fabric.

TO ADD THE DRAWSTRINGS:
17. Take the two 4 × 81.5cm (1½in × 32in) pink print strips and fold in half. Press to get a sharp fold line. Open out and fold each raw edge into the centre. Fold again so that the folded edges are on top of each other. Topstitch down each long side.

18. Attach a safety pin to the end of one drawstring and, starting on the right side, use the safety pin to pull the drawstring through the front casing and back through the back casing. Remove the safety pin and tie the ends in a knot on the right side. Repeat the process for the second drawstring but start on the left side.

HANDY HINTS:

• The length of the handles on this bag are just right for carrying your bag. If you would like to have longer handles so that you can put the bag over your shoulder, increase the length of each handle by another 30cm (12in).

• Choosing a bright contrasting fabric for the casing, drawstrings and handles gives the bag a real pop of colour.

ROTARY CUTTING

All the fabric pieces for the patterns in this book can be cut using a rotary cutter. If you are new to using a rotary cutter it is worth spending some time practising on scrap fabric as accuracy does improve with practice.

To cut safely, always hold the cutter firmly in your hand at a 45 degree angle and place your other hand on the ruler. The hand on the ruler needs to be flat with the fingers slightly opened, making sure that fingers are away from the edges of the ruler. Flip the safety cover off the cutter and place the blade next to the ruler. Starting at the bottom of the fabric begin to cut away from yourself until you have cut past the end of the fabric.(**A**).

The patchwork shapes in this book consist of squares, rectangles and triangles. All of these can be cut from strips of fabric that have been cut to specific widths.

Before you make your first cut, iron the fabric to remove any wrinkles. Fold the fabric selvedge to selvedge. If you use a 61cm (24in) long ruler you should not need to fold the fabric again but if your ruler is shorter you may need to fold the fabric again so that the fold is on the selvedge. Ensure that all the layers are smooth. Place the ruler firmly on top of the fabric and cut the selvedges from the fabric, tidying up any uneven edges.

To cut strips of fabric from which further shapes can be cut, align the even horizontal edge of the fabric with the first vertical measurement on the cutting board (**B**).

(A)

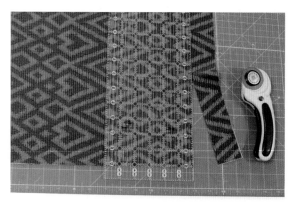

(B)

Close the safety cover on the cutter before putting the cutter down. It is easier to stand and cut rather than sit and a kitchen work surface is usually at an appropriate height.

Place the ruler on top so that the measurement you wish to cut is in line with the edge of the fabric. e.g. if you wish to cut a 5cm (2in) strip the 5cm (2in) marking of the ruler will be even with the cut edge of the fabric.

Line up the cutter with the ruler and cut away from yourself (**C**).

(C)

It is then easy to cut the strips into shapes for either the patchwork or the bag pieces. If you wish to cut squares, place the strip on the cutting board horizontally and then using the ruler vertically, measure the same width as the strip, keeping a ruler line on the long edge of the strip ensuring that a right angle is maintained and cross cutting the strip into squares (**D**). Rectangles can be cut in a similar manner.

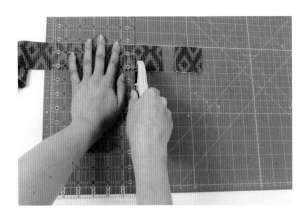

(D)

To cut right angled triangles, cut squares as described above and then cut the squares in half on the diagonal from corner to corner (**E**). Make sure that you hold the ruler firmly when cutting on the diagonal as it is easy to wobble and then the triangles will not be consistent in size.

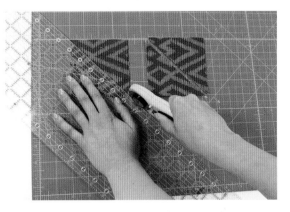

(E)

PATCHWORK TECHNIQUES

The patchwork techniques used in the bags in this book feature squares, rectangles, right angled triangles or flying geese-style triangles. All of the patchwork is stitched on the sewing machine. Each bag pattern explains how to stitch the shapes together and has photos to show the stages, but the step-by-step patchwork process is explained in more detail below:

Basic piecing techniques:

Basic piecing involves stitching two shapes together using a standard straight stitch on the machine. The raw edges of the shapes must be aligned precisely in order for the patchwork to be accurate.

Usually when patchwork piecing, you do not need to back stitch at the beginning of a seam, however for actual bag making this is essential. (More about this in the bag making section.) All seams are 0.75cm (¼in) wide.

If you have a patchwork foot on your sewing machine you can align the edge of the foot with the edge of the fabric to get an accurate seam. If you do not have a 0.75cm (¼in) patchwork foot you can adjust the needle position so that an accurate seam is achieved. (**A**).

(A)

To chain piece squares and rectangles:

If you have lots of squares or rectangles to stitch together you can chain piece the shapes together. Place the first two shapes right sides together, making sure that the edges to be stitched line up. Using the patchwork foot on the machine, line up the edge of the fabric with the edge of the foot.

Stitch along the seam line, but when you reach the end of the fabric, leave the needle down, lift the presser foot and slip the next two pieces to be stitched under the foot, leaving a small space between it and the previously stitched shapes.

Continue stitching in this way to make a chain of patchwork shapes. It looks just like patchwork bunting. Once you have stitched the pieces, cut them apart and continue to join the shapes together as needed (**B**).

(B)

To piece right-angled triangles:

These triangles are often called half square triangles. They are pieced by starting with squares. To stitch two triangles start with two squares, each in a different fabric. Draw a line on the diagonal, on the wrong side of one of the squares. Place the squares on top of each other with right sides facing and the edges aligned. (**C**) Stitch 0.75cm (¼in) on each side of the drawn diagonal line. Cut apart on the diagonal line (**D**) and press seams towards the darker fabric (**E** and **F**).

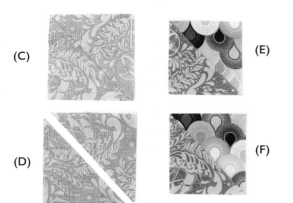

(C)

(E)

(D)

(F)

To piece flying geese triangles:

Method One

This method of stitching triangles is fast and also avoids having to stitch on a cut bias edge. It does however waste fabric as you are cutting off and discarding excess fabric. To make one flying geese unit you will need a rectangle and two squares cut to the appropriate measurement. Draw a line on the diagonal on the wrong side of each square. Position a square on one side of the rectangle, right sides facing, so that the drawn diagonal line travels from the bottom corner to the middle of the rectangle (**G**). Stitch on the drawn line. Trim away the excess fabric 0.75cm (¼in) from the stitching (**H**). Fold the triangle back and press (**I**). Repeat on the other side of the rectangle (**J**).

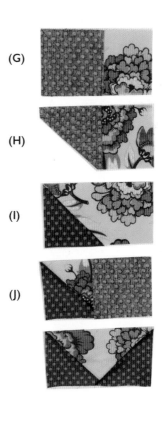

(G)

(H)

(I)

(J)

Method Two

This method starts with one large square in one fabric and four smaller squares in a second fabric. Draw a line on the diagonal on the wrong side of all the small squares. Position two small squares on diagonally opposite corners of the large square so that the drawn line is running from corner to corner and stitch 0.75cm (¼in) away from each side of the drawn line (**A**). Cut along the drawn line (**B**) and press seams towards the small triangles (**C**). Position the final two squares on the remaining unstitched corners of each unit so that the diagonal line is positioned between the two smaller triangles. Stitch a 0.75cm (¼in) seam away from each side of the drawn line (**D**). Cut along the drawn line (**E and F**) and press seams towards the small triangles. This produces four flying geese units (**G and H**).

(C)

(D)

(A)

(B)

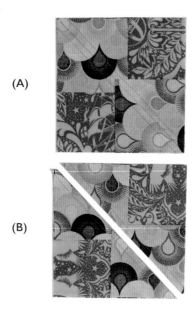

(E)

(F)

(G)

(H)

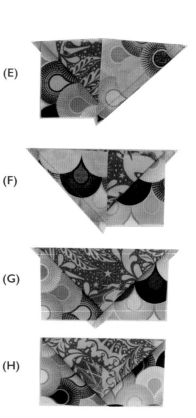

To match intersections:

It is important that seams match and points are sharp when piecing. When seams meet at an intersection make sure that the seam allowances are pressed in opposite directions.

The seam allowances should butt together and can be pinned through the stitching lines to hold the pieces in place before stitching. This same principle can be used when diagonal seams need to meet when stitching triangles together. I usually pin the patchwork shapes together by putting the pins in vertically to the stitching line rather than horizontally. The pins can then be removed just before the needle of the machine gets to the pin.

PRESSING

Pressing makes such a difference to the finished product in patchwork and bag making. A nicely constructed bag has a professional finish when pressed. To steam or not to steam with the iron? Personal preference here, but I always use a dry iron and never feel the need to use steam.

It is important to iron fabrics before cutting to make sure that all the wrinkles and creases are removed. All the seams in the bags in this book are pressed to one side. The only exception is if there is a very thick, bulky seam and where this occurs the seams are pressed open. If seams need to be pressed open the individual instructions for each bag tell you to do so. As you complete each stage of the patchwork or bag making it is important to press seams before moving on to the next step and adding another shape or strip of fabric. Where possible, try to press seams in one direction from the right side of the fabric towards the darker fabric. This helps to make sure that there are no little creases or folds in the seam line. Gently press the seams rather than using a backwards and forwards motion with the iron.

QUILTING

Some of the bags in this book are machine quilted while others are not quilted at all. The majority of the quilting is done on the outer bag with the exception of the clutch bag where the quilting takes place on the lining. Quilting does enhance the patchwork or fabric by giving the bag texture and the good thing about quilting a bag is that it is small and not as daunting as quilting a whole quilt.

If you have a walking foot for your sewing machine this will help to make the quilting easier. If you do not have a walking foot you can use an ordinary machine foot but you may want to reduce the thread tension on the machine. I like to quilt with a thread that either matches or compliments the fabric and will often use a thread with a sheen to emphasize the patchwork. Keep the thread in the bobbin a grey colour as it will not be seen and is hidden by the lining.

The quilting sandwich consists of the outer bag and fusible wadding (batting). All the bag patterns use fusible wadding as once this is fused to the fabric it makes it secure and pinning is not necessary. The quilting holds these two layers together before the lining is added to the inner bag. Sometimes it is necessary to mark the quilting lines on the fabric with a marker and at other times the quilting can be completed in a random fashion. If you need to mark straight lines on the fabric, use a ruler and mark the lines lightly. For some straight line quilting, the edge of the walking foot is all that is needed to ensure straight quilting lines.

BAG MAKING TECHNIQUES

The majority of bag making techniques are described in the step-by-step instructions however there are a few extras and reminders to help you on your way.

Seams:
Seams need to be secured at each end to stop them coming undone. When starting to stitch a seam, stitch forwards three stitches and then reverse over the stitches to secure before stitching the seam. Repeat the process at the end of each seam.

Stitching a curved seam:
It is important when stitching a curved seam to keep the stitching parallel to the edge of the fabric. After stitching, clip the curves at intervals before turning through. This will ensure that the seam lies flat and smooth.

Stitching the lining closed:
After the bags are turned through, the gap in the lining needs to be stitched closed. This can be done in either of two ways. If the gap is tucked out of sight you can carefully machine stitch the folded edges of the lining together with matching thread. If the gap is positioned in a place where it is more visible, carefully over sew the folded edges together by hand.

Adding extra pockets:
Many of the bags have pockets in the lining of varying sizes and each pattern describes how to add pockets. You may find that you wish to add extra pockets to the bag or change their sizes. This can be done easily when constructing the lining. Determine the size of the pocket to be added, check that the size of the lining will support the additional pocket and then follow the step by step instructions in the Spotty Dotty Messenger Bag pattern to stitch the pocket.

Adding haberdashery:

Adding bag fastenings, studs, straps, D rings or buckles gives a patchwork bag a very professional finish. There are a number of online suppliers where bag making haberdashery can be purchased. The bags featured have used various items of bag hardware as appropriate. Always follow the manufacturer's instructions when adding a fastening and measure twice before cutting the fabric for the insertion.

Acknowledgements

I have so enjoyed creating the projects and writing the patterns for this book and I am very grateful to everyone who played a part in the process. Many thanks to Darren and Georgina at Quail Studio for all their hard work, great design and endless patience. To Rowan Yarns and Lady Sew and Sew thank you for all the lovely fabrics and materials to work with.

Janet Goddard

SUPPLIERS
Coats Crafts UK (www.makeitcoats.com)
Lady Sew and Sew (www.ladysewandsew.co.uk)